FOREST BOOKS

SPRING TIDE

PIA TAFDRUP was born in Copenhagen in 1952. She took her degree at Copenhagen University in 1977 and her first published work appeared in the periodical *Chancen* in 1980. Between 1981 and 1988 she published six books of poetry and a play while also editing two anthologies of Danish poetry. Her poems have been translated for magazine publication into French, German, Swedish and English and she has received numerous scholarships for writing and travel.

ANNE BORN is a poet, translator and historian. Her last translations for Forest Books were Bo Carpelan's *Room Without Walls* and Solveig von Schoultz's *Snow and Summers*.

Pia Tafdrup

SPRING TIDE

by

PIA TAFDRUP

Translated from the Danish
by
ANNE BORN

FOREST BOOKS
LONDON ☆ 1989 ☆ BOSTON

Published by
FOREST BOOKS

20 Forest View, Chingford, London E4 7AY, U.K.
P.O. Box 438, Wayland, MA 01778, U.S.A.

First published 1989

Typeset in Great Britain by Cover to Cover, Cambridge
Printed in Great Britain by BPCC Wheatons Ltd, Exeter

Translations © Anne Born
Original poems © Pia Tafdrup
Cover design © Ann Evans
Introduction © Ove Ancker
Photograph © Gregers Nielsen

British Library Cataloguing in Publication Data
Tafdrup, Pia
Spring tide: selected poems of Pia Tafdrup
I. Title   II. Born, Anne
839.8'1172

ISBN No 0–948259–55–8

Library of Congress Catalogue Card No. 89–80341

FOREST BOOKS gratefully acknowledges the financial support of
the Danish Ministry of Culture
and wishes to thank Borgen's Forlag, Copenhagen, who first
published *Spring Tide* in Danish in 1985, for their co-operation,
and Farnau, Straus & Giroux for permission to quote from
Osip Mandelstam's *Selected Poems*.

Contents

Introduction
The Language of Desire

'Poesie ist ein Zustand der Sprache.' Pia Tafdrup introduces her fourth poetry collection with this aphorism by Helmut Heissenbüttel. With *Spring Tide* she achieves the poetic maturity and clarity implicit in her earlier collections which here are fully realised. From the title and through epigraphs to the seven sections, the collection is carried along on a generous singing rhythm which gives expression to undescribed areas of the female body and psyche. *Spring Tide* is a book about desire, a sustained attempt to record in poetry the different forms and states of desire.

The title, *Spring Tide*, denotes the highest tide at new and full moon, and through this phenomenon Pia Tafdrup links the cycle of nature with the female cycle and the cycle of desire. This all-pervading rhythm of rising and falling carries the poem sequence through the seven sections and creates a form for the various interests and studies in sex, body, time, language and the world.

The central section of *Spring Tide* consists of 28 poems and interweaves several cycles — of the moon, woman, desire and the year. From poem to poem the section moves towards climax, which occurs at the same time as ovulation and which denotes passion's culmination in orgasm, and introduces various states into the language of poetry, after which the waning moon takes over and leads on towards menstruation and desire's acceptance of death. But this pattern is merely a major rhythm carrying the individual poems. There are none of the menstruation poems of the 70s in this section, only a constant investigation of language and the body. Thus the moon is merely a metaphor for time, while the images for desire are the sun and leaping fire. All very classical, yet astonishingly new and revealing.

In her earlier collections, *When an angel's been grazed*, *No-hold* and *The innermost zone*, Pia Tafdrup sought to express in poetry unconscious or unknown regions of the body and consciousness. She developed an impressive ability to describe the smallest and most overlooked details in precise and crystal-clear images. She has retained this technique, but in *Spring Tide* laid less emphasis on precise formulation in favour of concentration on rhythm and pulse, inspired by her own performance readings. The poems in *Spring Tide* are thus intimately linked with voice and breathing, and the reader will gain extra pleasure in reading the poems aloud and so feeling the movement of the rhythm. And constantly there is this fantastic talent for synthesising a whole sense perception into a single vibrating compressed word, as in the poem 'April earth', in which everything is epitomised in the sensations of the fingertips.

From the start of her writing Pia Tafdrup has emphasised the body as the source of sensation. But this concentration on bodily experiences, including those of the female cycle and desire, does not exclude the universe. On the contrary, *Spring Tide* begins and ends with an opening out, which has roots in the physical but which creates a connection between the individual and the world. The first section of *Spring Tide* contains the long, supremely accomplished poem, 'Exalted for birth', which discusses our natural condition as human beings, including among other things desire and birth. But see how the perspective is extended to embrace commitment — at first to the sexual but then further to the whole world:

> but without desire
> our bodies are not real bodies
> without children
> the world is no longer the world
> and without longing for the moment
> when all around us has vanished
> when obliterating ourselves in forgetfulness
> pure and beautiful as snow
> becoming water
> when birds start to call
> to other birds
> no continuation is possible
> no elevation for birth possible

Against the background of this understanding of what is central in human life, in the seventh and final section Pia Tafdrup can confront rearmament and threats of war and formulate a protest not primarily grounded in a political attitude, but which shows that destruction is maladjustment and rearmament a threat to life itself. In the long powerful poem, 'The four cradles', she demonstrates how modern society attacks children, with the symbols of four cradles representing idyll, conformism, rearmament and death. The perspective opens out on to society but the opening starts from within.

Again and again *Spring Tide* reveals the hidden connections between the individual and the surrounding world, between desire and nature, between moment and eternity, but at the same time the book emphasises that these connections do not simply exist but are the realised result of a concentration which leads to perception and insight. The interconnections are the product of linguistic effort, they are brief glimpses of insight which establish momentary connections and allow individuals to feel themselves as a beat in a more complex rhythm. These gentle, ecstatic experiences are the goal, the moment, in which conception takes place, when there is total surrender.

Spring Tide is a consistent, coherent work of art in which the various elements seem bound together by an interior power. Throughout the collection there are innumerable inner lines of connection between the sections despite the fact that their subject matter diverges in theme from the natural meaning of life, the connection between the moon and the egg, natural cycles, pain and time, language and society. The individual poems investigate their specific sphere with a sure touch and form part of the whole through their overall perceptions, images and rhythm. And throughout the book flows this vast, rocking pulse, which transports the reader to a poetic condition of language in which the moment seems to become eternal, in which the tides of poetry break through all dams.

Ove Ancker
Lecturer in Danish
Language and Literature

The Syntax of Desire

Spring Tide, my fourth collection, is the one that has attracted most readers. The title refers to the highest tide at full and new moon. I have sought to transpose these maximum fluctuations to the body. It is a book on the nature of passion. Not a documentary description but an attempt to speak of desire in images and music. All the many forms of desire are depicted, from the states of tenderness and devotion to situations when reason retreats before purely animal instinct. I have tried not merely to write *about* desire but to a great degree demonstrate it. The poems must have body. They themselves are sign and physiology, rhythm and pulse. I have tried to write the syntax of desire, to search out and formulate the life of the body. I wished to write about what is hard to understand, about the not yet thought, but sensed. My poems are not solutions, but questions.

Pia Tafdrup

Poesie ist ein Zustand der Sprache
(Poetry is a condition of language)

Helmut Heissenbüttel

I

I have the present of a body — What should I do with it,
so unique it is and so much mine?

Osip Mandelstam

Elevated to birth

Perhaps no tomorrow
and yet always
the longing for that moment
when cells at last will take
their dumb decision
on non-growth or growth and regrowth
that moment
when hovering in nothingness
we are dissolved in colours from within
crashing quivering fainting
like birdsong
early in March
that moment
when cells' sparks
shine in the night
the ever dangerous
deep close night
that moment
when cells' fire
consumes the fear
that holds back life and relife
has always held back
but never so much as now
when none dares
talk of continuance
perhaps because never before
has it been
so unpredictable
never before
so threatened

but without passion
our bodies aren't real bodies
without children
the world no more the world
and without longing for that moment
when all blanks out around us
when extinguishing ourselves in oblivion
pure and beautiful as snow
that turns to water
when birds start to call

2

to other birds
no continuance is possible
no elevation for birth possible

Perhaps nothing tomorrow
and yet always
the longing for that moment
when our bodies yield
and we let ourselves be borne
through infinite space
those seconds
when we taste the sound
of silence

Doch alle Lust will Ewigkeit!
will tiefe, tiefe Ewigkeit —

3

II

Each movement
must come from within ourself
water is there
for us all

Göran Sonnevi

The moon

It's true
that the course of the moon
the egg in my body
are more than an event
in language
that the unseen
makes everything more visible.

seeing

Correspondence

The semantic moon
exchanges letters
with the left ovary

the cold a white hand
that attacks
blind, but sure

the cold a white hand
that clenches and opens
in darkness

an ash pearl
is thrust out into night
listening to the rising sea.

The same gaze

Through greyblack clouds
the moon comes out
with its cold light
    blindly looking
    among the living
    and the dead

the same gaze
a drowning bird sends
towards the flock in the air

Procession

Wake late at night
when the chill comes
and snails ooze
up the steps

my darkness
and the moon's own moondarkness

white dwarves with little dolls
advance in a quiet procession
with sealed letters
sent from other lands
dragging bags and carriers
full of pearls
long swaying lines of figures
slow on bare feet
through the empty street
in flickering silvery light
    neverborn children
    stare
    into my eyes.

Dråben

I dråben
mister
et insekt
sit liv

i havet
taber
en måne
sig selv

afstanden
til død
er aldrig
længere væk
nd tæt på.

The drop

In the drop
an insect
loses
its life

in the sea
a moon
loses
itself

the distance
to death
is never
further
than close to.

Halfsleep images

Life must reach
beyond dream borders
so I want the body now
quivering light in each cell

it's what
isn't visible
that reflects itself
clearest
the unsaid
certainly hears the body
and understands

so all halfsleep pictures
must grow in the wild
imagination's plasma flow
between the heart's rose-grey walls
only thus
can we do everything

I count moonphases
and feel
space and seconds
I am part
of the cycle
a piece of nature
that won't die
until I've lived
with the sun in my mouth.

III

O Wealth, in which I swim —
Sun-sleep, in which I dream!

Thøger Larsen

Whisper and hope

Not east not west
rather the blood's aim
towards the sun
or the dream of the sun
perhaps just the dream of the
dream state.

April earth

Steaming April earth smelled
through streams of shifting grey
and in the transparent forest edge
rustling dry straws from last year
snapped pale in the new grass
again rays of sunlight that settle
like beating colours behind the eyes
or strike home into the brain
again April quivering fingertips
and the free fall of sudden thoughts
again the urge to offer
seconds of a vibrating morning.

Hear you call

See a sinking sun, on its head
kiss your hands

flow through the dark
                          alone
fall over in wet grass
                          freezing
among silent tense plants
hear you call
will not listen
what is it
you want
what is it
I want

between beat and beat
                          from the heart
press deeper down
                          into earth that yields
among chopping vomit
                          put down roots in a spring
alone freezing from the heart into earth that
                          puts down roots in a spring.

If the light doesn't

Your fingers
    for the first time
over my face
    a touch
I could feel
for days

no life
    without expectation
no leap
    without take-off
no long
        fall
without the jump
your fingers
    for the first time, slow
    movements
I could feel
for days
all else unreal

warmth
insists

no joy
    rising song
to break into
if the light doesn't
reach into my rooms
and stand still
like columns of sun
if your eyes don't
make me let go of everything

only one time
    is the first
but I dream of longer days
with you

your fingers
     caressing everything around you
make me see
     what they can do to me
there's a rushing in my breast
a rushing in my breast

your fingers
so careful
and yet
the blood's throbbing surge

a leaping flood of joy

your lips
first searching

your tongue's dragging trail upon my neck.

Further still

What has not been
will come
    you know it
    I know it
    you know I know
    I know you know I know
you whisper me into
ecstasy
in
where I can see
far as in dreams
and further still

could not have lived
without your words
without your hands everywhere, your mouth
these journeys towards light
where we celebrate the seconds

you whisper me into
ecstasy
like the sun sensed
behind closed eyelids
you whisper me into
ecstasy
and further still
    this is what I live for
you whisper oblivion
of all else
whisper forth salt
in the corners of my eyes
faint rustling of skin

sing blood sing lips
your throat
and the pits of your shoulders
fires on open squares
— absolutely still
    behind all words
behind all writing
the desire
for desire.

The room filled

The light changes
I lay a hand
on your shoulder

on the wall struck
by the sun
falls the shadow
of a bird

your life
and my life
black on white
inwardly filled
with colours
up over the bare plane

you turn
towards me
all is reality

the shadow rises on the wall
and vanishes
the room is filled with wings
your life and mine

Living turned

Sparks carried
on crackling fingers
fire in hands' bare palms
fire in flat dishes

searched for your eyes
in distant places
let word on word
point towards you

then you suddenly see me
across all thoughts' distance
then you suddenly hear me
and it's you
drawing me to you
you putting an arm
round my shoulders
you pulling me
closer in
me cautiously
stealing an arm around you
you whose hard grasp
takes hold of my neck
presses me
closer and closer in

so turned to each other
in a place far off and close to
the world can go on falling apart
in slow and continuous decay
so turned to each other
you feel my body everywhere
vibrate ever tense
I feel your body everywhere
so living turned to each other
a new sun rolls
across the sky
new light falls
amongst rubble of stones.

Between bird and bird

Fiery shreds in the air
roots of my glittering flesh
a bird's song
to another
another bird's song
to a third
and so on.

It's between
tree and tree
the notes are set free
and flames pierce shrill

between tree and tree
an invisible shield of song surges
a quivering rootnet of sparkling voices
stretched in the air

it's between
bird and bird
in empty space
the seconds tick in my flesh.

The skin

The skin my only limit
pass it where
light is strongest
don't shut the world out
or me in

show me
that the sun in the sky
is the dream within me
the burning reality
when you bite holes
and let me feel
there are no differences
between outside and inside
between pain and caress
stone and word

I am the one
who porous to your caprice
opens in desire
everywhere and all at once
to exist in the world

give me what you have
of everything
I ask
for no more.

The voice

In the room
       a voice
between walls between
floor and ceiling
between walls and ceiling between
walls and floor
       a voice
like glass filled
by your shining hand
       with wine
pure red streaming
the blood in all its colours

in the room
       a voice
close to my ear
like a beginning
of something I've not yet known

I have made my heart big
and listen
to the voice
       that is yours
a glass that is emptied
by my joyful lips

a magnetic distance from my ear
I hear
your voice in the room

I have made my heart big
and await you
between walls between floor and ceiling
in a circle of light
in an ecstasy
of golden drops
the body waits
in my body.

My naked body

Drops of sun
splashes of flame
light cutting a way
one early morning
sprays hard rays
against my naked body
that plays burning-glass
to the highest leaping fire.

The sun

Have drunk a lot
eaten and said
much of this
and that and whispered
                    your blood
                    your clouds
                    your dreams in red

drunk and trembling revealed
something or other and probably far too much
specially about red dreams
gently licked your ear wet and whispered
nothing and everything
felt an arm round my shoulder
arms hold my body fast
hands and fingers clutch my hair
felt eyes seize mine
seen and mirrored — mirrored and seen
domes of light
invisible rays luring
heat in the womb
the urge to grasp harder
the urge to swaying dizzying
be held harder
the urge to sail
into the colours of the heavens
surge right into a sky crackling shining

have drunk and waited
                    hours
for these minutes I
and you
seize and seize
and you have waited
                    hours
for these minutes
and your mouth
sees now
the sun
between my legs
                    swaying seconds in the body.

Spring tide

Spring tide
>> I lie down
>> bare myself
>> I'll be your animal
>> for a moment
>> with senses stretched out
>> between neck and heel

spring tide
>> my body's an arc of desire
>> I turn a shoulder
>> strain my head back

spring tide
>> my throat's free
>> and you can smell the blood beneath the skin
>> I dare to be your animal a moment

spring tide
>> I can shine everywhere

spring tide
>> I can open myself everywhere

spring tide
>> you can do what you want with me everywhere

spring tide
>> I am nearer the sun everywhere
>> pure drops of light
>> in a growing abyss of lust.

Wetted the heavens

Have whispered your blood hotter
than shimmering summers
wetted the heavens in your skin
sluiced my water into your orifices
licked salt from stone
glistening surfaces
slipped urgent words
fragments
            of shining sound
in among your stars
with my feet
trampled and kneaded your soft soil
with my hands in your water
sluiced myself
breathed secretions
spraying rapture
                and screams
with my body chopped my way in
to your country
            in fear of death
slobbering raving
let myself hurl
out into black space.

For a moment

With strangely flaring filaments
with the blood black circling
with the sun in my mouth
    brute and angel
        in one body.

Behind desire

The peace sometimes
    in subjecting yourself
to something
that's greater
than you
in submitting
    to those images
    that now and then
    threaten
    to turn up
on the other side
of desire
submitting
    to dissolution
without resistance
submitting
    to what is the reality
behind desire
    to the splintering white
moment of annihilation
when the earth
opens.

Late rays

The sun's late rays
corrode evening
in my skin, copper
and the blood rolls into
a larger sky
where colours wash upwards
and calmly flow over.

So much

So much you demand
so little
so often
and all too seldom

luckily
we don't always understand
what it is we want

but I'm still alive
I still have words

    am not just holes
   to be filled
  with wine
        with seed
             with sun
and emptied again bright and quivering

August sky

The summer askew
with festering wounds
swallows in flocks spread
over a barleyfield pus yellow

scudding dive and lift and soar
black chips in the air
a strange jabbing dance one with another
free flying
in the same great invisibly staked out field
writing on the wall of the sky
wing knife in space
leaping script for a chance reader
one late afternoon of wind
while vein grey thunderclouds
part
for a strip of sun
over whipping springboards
matter flows free
from the bubbling tissue
seething golden August.

Burning point

The body is ever body
    black sparkling
and lust the same
    sun and wild fire
the blood
    quick stabbing knives
I kiss your closed eyelids
kiss your parted lips
lick your burns
    kiss and lick
    cutting softly

we'll be greedy once more, we'll
gather all shining rays
cling to each other closer closer
hurl ourselves into flowing golden rhythms
hurl ourselves into giddy depths
singing seething rapture
when trembling and slowly we
    burn up from deep inside.

On the edge

Our lit bodies
talked of possible
limits and we were
recklessly alive
somewhere softly near
the heart's fiery region
we were flesh with all nights
on the longest night close to greedy brutes
when we came out to the edge where the world was
and the words wanted to leave us just there
not come to a sudden stop wanted
further further still but
crashed themselves against
a wall of white the
poem can speak now
about sparkling
silence.

Being

In strange places
you pursue me
dripping fire
in every cleft
you invade
the land behind the skin

bird in the sky
flickering, snickering
in hurling flight

dripping fire
in every cleft
is it you
uniting us
with pain

bird from the sky
whirling down
through the air

then you see a face
open quiet
silent as a sea
one raingrey morning

the bird strikes
a stone on the shore

then you see a bird's head
almost cut from a bird's body

the state
of being in the world

my flesh
of blood and rust
the smell of metal
everywhere.

The forest

Leaves roll around themselves
trees rest
in dozing selflessness

the forest strolls about
in a rust embroidered dress
in its scented swishing lacy dress
with wound borders
walks with slow steps
down towards a harvest field
rests its sick hands
on a fence
before painting its nails
red brown yellow
red brown yellow

the forest fired by the sun
shines
not gold
not autumn
but already the summer dead
low sunrays on leaves
bonfire in rarely seen colours.

Shadows in the blood

The fire in the earth
burns in the body
my nights
are flowing hot stones
my days spiced
with ashes
my tissue burns down
in exposed places

the fire in the earth
burns in the body
my shadows grow
in the blood
arise
both vitally black and strange
slowly start to move
grow so disturbingly alive
now as I shrink up
freezing in the sun's last rays.

Pneumo

September fever
and frail
moments before the dark
chill fields
against the sky's pleura
    inflamed rose flush
as in a newborn child
dissected warm by a quiet knife

September fever
coupled with dry coughing
ash brittle crusts
porous harrowed fields
with occasional trees
where the first twilight birds
settle down
    alive
on fragile nerve fibres.

Related to darkness

So close to a presence
that quivers when I quiver
dances when I dance
without faltering
follows me in everything
never bars the way
or hinders my whim

so close to a presence
related to darkness
and therefore related
to the darkness itself

no gap between the shadow and me
no acid spray
of reproaches in the air
no strife
to tear up an afternoon
into thin fluttering strips
of fleeting sorrow

so close to a presence
I can never hide from
never hide behind
so close to a presence
and yet not be seen
so close to
without it ever
managing to change me.

Matter

Made of that matter
that glows in the sun
I'm reflected
by a long shadow
that whispers in a thousand tongues:

you yourself will fall to earth
alien to all
that lives.

All is

All is reality
in the end white
darkness.

IV

Everything we fix is already past.
No one can twice descend into the same river of light.

Werner Aspenström

Bergen

Only today is today
cold and clear
and if it rains tomorrow
and the days after
no one will understand
how the sun in late September
towards evening
can throw its shadows
against Bergen's mountain walls
so they break
into purple inflammations
and celestial pink
turn the town into
a northern Athens

tomorrow today is yesterday
and no one will remember
that in my wanderings
along these steep streets
I throw strange shadows
on the steps between houses

when to imitate
this light
that's so exactly
like secretions
from a vast brain
I double up and spit
blood and starsplinters.

Firmament

Firmament crystal
crushed
to fine dust
that roughly grinds
all mucous membranes

back to coals and night
back to quiet birds

to space deep down
where the dark flows
forth new planets
in slow dance.

Singing glass

Thin rays
         of fear
at first hurting badly
                  like glass
that sings till it shatters
in the finest vessels
till it breaks
             in a thousand sharpcutting splinters

then the feel
         of nothing
but frost
jerking quietly
at the nerves' tenderest threads.

Needles

Needles
in my flesh

silverminers' veins
deep in the earth

the blood black icing up
in its tracks

behind all understanding
only one heart

that can refuse
to beat.

Sleep years

At the bottom of the city
where life oozes through the walls
I see myself
one cold morning
alone
at the table
with my hands
grey-yellow as hay moving
the cup around the table
seeing myself
stare into a wall
behind the first of my dying
bones
seeing myself
let a needle
seeing my fingers' random movements
all over the table
seeing myself
let a needle
slide slowly
under a
nail
with its silent pain.

This house

Walls without doors
in this house
ceilings without cracks
infinite distances
between tenderness and tenderness
between my words
                    and you

listen to weariness
all that
never gets said
silent while forgetting

listen to notes
from the trembling dark
in the body
at midday

wait
from somewhere or other
for black rain
that can wash
                    wounds clean.

A fall into yourself

A feather on the water
sails night
into the wet tissue of the brain

dreams in
to the growing dark
ships hung in dank cathedrals

drifts like snow falling
under a lamp in the street
reeling hypnotic silent.

V

nights wet with silence and peace
windows open to blueshadows' snow

Søren Ulrik Thomsen

Frost letter

My dear

Last night
there was a frost
and this morning snow from the southeast
it fell so quietly
almost imperceptibly
as only the first snow of the year
comes sinking
suddenly white
and made us talk
with voices
turned differently
towards each other
with words fetched
from last winter

It was a wonderful morning
better than I've had for a long time
Hooray for the snow!
yelled my son
as he leapt
from chair to chair
from window to window
for you can't walk on the floor
when it's snowing
so suddenly white
you know that

We're in for a winter like 66
snow right up to April
said the postman handing me the paper
I promised him a beer
if he was right
— in April, that is . . .

My dear, the whole day has been so amazing
in the evening I was reading Frank O'Hara
who has always spoken so clearly
to the shadows in my blood
when I suddenly saw him

smile at me from his picture
only twenty-five years old
you wouldn't believe
how happy I felt

My dear, it's far too long
since I heard from you
if you get snowed in
perhaps you'll have time to write?
if the winter really goes on
from November to April
how many letters
we'd get written —
if only it stays frozen
for good.

With all best wishes.

Snow

Through a hole
in the snow
see the snow
as snow
observe a world
larger than the world
can see no beginning
no ending
find only myself
staring
into an eternity's eye
deciphering a silence
white and transparent.

Only my blood

Fields have no names
are not remembered like streets
each one of them
only as calm stretches
in the thick of the day's unrest

turn the winterface
to the sun above the wood
feel the heart
beating hard
stand with half-closed eyes
and the wind in my back
turned away from all
I know
stand still there
where the snowfields run down
to the wood
where nothing else is seen through the eyelashes
where animal tracks
cross each other
in deep blue
where they have carved holes in the snow
or into drifts
in the lee of hedges
and hidden themselves for a while

stand quite still   .
and feel time dissolving
the wind
that's cold
the sun
that's warm
        like this
the world's simple
it's just I
who don't know
what I want
it is only my blood
that runs
in all directions
a multibranched movement

that makes it so hard
to choose between words
to decide
on just one life.

Melon seller on a winter's day

Another day of snow
when everything's stopped
when Europe freezes
including a man
who wants to sell me a whole mountain
of green melons
or just a single melon
or at the least
a juicy red slice

who shouting
felt nothing else
than his own loud voice around the walls
on a day when sun rained down
in the streets of Rome
from a clear sky
hard onto my bare shoulders
on a day when his voice cut
shining through the street
like the knife
in fibrous flesh

I wonder is he ploughing his way past
the houses now
in a half empty street
or stopping somewhere
in snow up to his knees
to listen
to the silence of crystals
as if he had no ears to hear with
until this winter
when white is so white
had no eyes to see with
until the day he saw the children sledging
on the slope before the Colosseum

I throw a green shawl
round my shoulders
to keep the last drops of summer sun
a little longer
the scent of the fruit I ate.

White evening

White evening between us
silent hours with slow snow
lying on the roofs of the town

filling the streets
filling this room
the pits in my shoulders

your dog huddles against you
stands quietly with lowered head
closed eyes

your hand strokes his wet fur
that smells so strong
and pungent

I give myself time to think
it's good you don't always know
what it is you want

white evening between us
quiet hours with slow snow
covering the bark of my brain

the blood I drink
makes all distance unreal
gives fire to my eyes, you say suddenly.

Greater than the snow

A silence
like bushes
breaking out into white

a tenderness
like snow
melting on the face

a caress
whose light impression
is the shape of unfathomable sorrow

greater
than the snow that streams
from an ever denser sky

greater
than eternal snow high in the mountains
the white peaks far distant from language.

If death . . .

As you can wake up
to a world
        covered with snow
you should be able to wake
to a death
that came
        just as quiet, just as slow

if death
could fall like snow
        wipe out a face like snow
come like something
that opened out
                in white
and at the same time closed
no one need fear
those strange gentle strokings
over eyelids and cheeks
that turn the thought
of death
into a bird

which flutters up scared
out of its shelter
                in the heart
so mysteriously real

VI

If only each person's unconfined voice
sings a new song
to infinity! The way to conquer victory!
It's only possible
in listening's note, sharply ringing

Göran Sonnevi

Capsule

Turn off
from the straight streets of language
flakes of grey sounds

make my way in
at a distance from the houses
to try the words for myself

circle towards
a spring's new buds
on our walk through town

practise a new way of walking
with my winter coat thrown
loosely round my shoulders

a capsule in black which opens
to our night
acidly scented with young wine.

Weightless

You can hover in language
hold yourself up
— horizontally —
for a while

pull out whirring words
from the grey inside of the brain

move
from nothing to nothing
without getting wet feet

for a weightless moment
sense
the space around the words

I speak
therefore I hover.

As late as today

Just a Country Town, 21 October 1984

The Intuition of the News
In just a Country Town
    Emily Dickinson

For Sys Hindsbo

Chinks of time
with grapes in water and wine
black olives layered with rosemary
with hectic heat
and shining words
with scurrying clouds
blown across open fields
and Emily Dickinson
queen without a crown
fluttering white
in among the trees
where apples fall
into trembling grass
talking awkwardly softly
and pale in the chill
about something she has lost
but always felt.

Between kerbstone and lightlines

The streets are stone
    and water
the pavements gravel
    and soft clay
in district after district
    the houses fall
around us
    or lie like deserted backdrops
from the century's wildest film
    but the wind is still
wind with strong
    soft gusts
when it meets us
on great muddy building sites
or where streets
cross streets
and we walk
over huge lakes
balance between kerbstone
and lightlines
from the rays of swinging lamps
    talking   talking   talking
of everything
    that can be spoken here
where the young women smell
stronger than hemlock
and the men paint
the shadows in their faces darker
the younger they are
    talking   talking   talking
carried away by each other's voices
    on a strangely springlike December night
between closed gateways and high railings
before houses of crumbling wood
    where you suddenly stop
because you hear me
    speak your name
as you have never heard it spoken before
    because you say
it's like getting

a completely new name
    when I speak it
that's what you
want to be called
    you say
that's how you want to be undressed
with a word
    I realise
and whisper you naked in your own name
in the lee of the houses
    held close to you
again and again
till you hold me
    just as close
as I want
you to hold me
while I give you your name
so you'll never
forget it again
    and feel
that now you're mine.

Each poem

Each word I have a feather
that shines
like the heart in a body

each sentence I have a wing
that brushes me like your glance
making me forget all else

each poem I have a bird
that takes off and searches the air
and throws me back to a new beginning

a word is a feather is a wing is a bird in flight.

Air and watersign

Set my mark
on the bird
and let it fly

set my mark
on the fish
and let it swim in the river

I have seen you both
loved you
for what you are
loved you the moment
you vanished

springbird
and
springfish

I can sing a long time now
of fire
of water

of what lives
within
of what marks
a person.

Words

A person
who speaks
has few sounds only
to make himself understood
and
within
all
words
is found
that blind
spot
called

silence

VII

Aus tiefem Traum bin ich erwacht!
(From deep dreams am I awakened!)

Nietzsche

The four cradles

For Ola Eustad's four cradles (1983)*

The cradle IDYLL
rock   blue   rock   silver
pulls down stars
for the sleeping child
the cradle IDYLL
imitates moonlight
in the darkest nights
in the cradle IDYLL
the quilt's a cloud
and the pillow the whitest wing
the fluffy sheet
is printed with gentle hymns
in the cradle IDYLL
the child is wrapped in cottonwool
shielded from the world
the rattle made of flowers
spreads soothing scents
the cradle IDYLL
rock   blue   rock   silver
rocks blessed dreams
into the frailest flickering sleep
who dares wake the little one?

The cradle CONFORMISM
swings in blue and warning orange
never a passion
never a desire
always casualness
straight social lines
in the cradle CONFORMISM
lies a child
who will fall asleep
to the striped signals of warning signs
the cradle CONFORMISM
is stuffed with brown envelopes

* Ola Eustad is a sculptor who gave the four cradles their names.

papers with endless rows of numbers
in the cradle CONFORMISM
the child keeps twitching like an animal
at last rests
dozes a moment
but then moans and whimpers again
who will listen to one
that calls in the dark?

The cradle FULL MOBILISATION
never keeps still
the cradle FULL MOBILISATION
is produced at the cavalry school of arms
with rockers of steel
the cradle FULL MOBILISATION
can march on the spot
one   two — one   two
till night becomes child
wrapped in green uniform
and the cradle's made
of leaves and branches
and the child will sleep
in a nest of leaves and mud
one   two — one   two
in the cradle FULL MOBILISATION
the child carries a little gun
one   two — one   two
the cradle FULL MOBILISATION
marches camouflaged
one   two — one   two
at night the child is beaten
because it won't sleep
at night the child won't sleep
because it's frightened
one   two — one   two
who will comfort a panicking child?

The cradle FINAL SOLUTION
clatters on the planks
of the bare floor
in the cold nursery

the cradle FINAL SOLUTION
is a little black casket
on creaking rockers
the naked child
in the cradle FINAL SOLUTION
rolls from side to side
bumps against the rough boards
with a dull sound that calls to mind
a soft stone
under the lid
the cradle FINAL SOLUTION
rocks to and fro
the cradle FINAL SOLUTION
rocks dead
and stands still
who said
dreamtime's gone?
What's
already happened?

Suspicion

Carefully laid by
hidden away
suddenly shadows
slip out

some days
all movement
can seem impossible
what is it
we fear

almost paralysed
what is it
we can't run from

laid aside
hidden away
slips out
pushes forward
grows bigger
what is it that unavoidably
attacks from within
breaks sinews
from within

thoughts assume
protective clothing

faces turned aside
quietly look round
open themselves
are forced to look

what is mutual
other than fear

how long can
mutual fear
postpone destructions

so long as fear
is in everyone
so long can we be forced
to think about it
so long . . .

but the day one says without fear
that in vain
he has run from everything
possible
that everything
laid aside
hidden away
will yet appear
that evil
and the urge to destroy
is what we fear in ourselves . . .

Hidden

A door is closed quite quietly
when those who decide make an error
When you feel that perhaps they are wrong
either because they know no better
don't want to know
or because they can't themselves
bring dreams into the world

When those who decide
may know themselves they are wrong
When you're convinced they know
that they're wrong but nevertheless
decide on the wrong standpoint
for a brief moment perhaps decide
on the easiest solution

When the resolve means
that the decision *is* taken
A movement stopped
Why then bother about it
Doesn't it only remind you
of something already
all too familiar?

A door closes quite quietly
How much in this world
isn't grounded on errors?
How many doors
aren't both closed and locked?

At first anger
then a mist of sorrow
a voice that breaks
and grows thin
Disappointment
and then the hidden
Curse
Revenge
Fingers that make signs
in the air
The day is not ended.

The impossible

We live with the impossible
chance happenings

everything that happens
is real

the cloud of gas
hanging
thick
and yellow over the town
where people are suffocatingly close
to unmoving
or frantically seek shelter
with each other

nothing is more real
than news that suddenly
pulverises the body's cells

nothing is more real
than anything else
the cloud of gas
is no hallucinated idea
we live with the impossible

war psychologists correct   calculate
make detailed notes
of a population in crisis

their observations
are no less real
than this poem

we live with the impossible
chance
and all its elements
we believe in the apparently
hopeless solutions, what hasn't been found
                    before,
— but which perhaps may come . . .

Epoch

We call it epoch
and think
never before
have there been such vicissitudes
so quick so unforeseen
never before
has our knowledge been made up
of scraps flakes of ash
never before
has it been so impossible to speak
of a unifying force

slow change
is now coup after coup
regulations already imposed
decisive resolutions made with force
cases brought long ago
go on and on
whether we will or no

and then I read in Sophus Claussen
in a note that he left
'What more miracles can be demanded of the Poets?
We live in a Period of concentrated World History,
as in an inferno of burning Planets,
a Nebula of enormous Deeds and Examples,
with which we are not yet satisfied.'

The sky is still the sky
the wind blows at the open window
the curtains move lightly
calm cool dusk
with pheasants shouting from the wood's edge
sound of a car starting
sound of a car driving past
the water in my glass
soon drunk
like the day
the past days and the months

here is a day
swallowed down and absorbed into the blood
with its special light
its seething drops of sound
its own smell
and firm hold on me

here is a day
which after all won't come again
here is a moment
in the file of moments
one given never to return
co-existing with the eternal return of being
in an inferno of burning planets
a nebula of enormous deeds . . .

War

Increased militarisation
of space
just means
that war comes nearer
the Centre
that the aim is
straight
for the Heart.

Vanishing days

It's not just spruce and pine
but the silence between the trees when the wind drops
that makes the silence greater
more transparent

it's not just grass and heather
but the sound that's lulled among the plants
that makes the evenings different from other evenings
light as downy feathers

it's not just dunes and miles
but the boom of steps on sandy ground
that travels through hard rocks
makes the substratum seem strangely hollow

it's not just the sea and wind
but the salt on my lips
that stings sharp and burning
and makes the tongue aware of landscape

it's not just the colours here
but the scent of colours when light changes
that goes on and goes on
in *one* infinity

it's not just the glow round honeysuckle and bluebell
but the thin flowing light on everything
that gives the best ecstasy
like the air I breathe

it's not just the afterglow here
but also the boundaries
growing uncertain
like the distance from dream to dream

it's not just hours that go fast and all too slow
but days that vanish
although the nights are shorter and lighter
than in any other place

it's not just untouched moments
but death
that's seen more clearly
here in this very place.

Other titles in the International Poetry Series
are available from: FOREST BOOKS,
20 Forest View, Chingford, London E4 7AY, U.K.